Religious Education in the Junior Years

Ralph Gower

A LION PAPERBACK

Tring · Belleville · Sydney

Copyright © 1984 Ralph Gower

Published by
Lion Publishing plc
Icknield Way, Tring, Herts, England
ISBN 0 85648 844 5
Albatross Books
PO Box 320, Sutherland, NSW 2232, Australia
ISBN 0 86760 574 X

First edition 1984

The author wishes to make
clear that the views expressed
in this book are his own,
and not necessarily those
of the Greater London
Council or the Inner London
Education Authority

Printed and bound in Great Britain by
Cox & Wyman, Reading

CONTENTS

PREFACE

I was asked recently if I would be seeking another job, at a higher level, with greater influence.

The question made me realize afresh that for me, the most fulfilling, satisfying and joyful work is to be working in the place I believe I ought to be. And I believe that that place is to help teachers to develop their skills in the teaching of religious education and to support them in all that they do.

What I can actually do in this respect is limited by time and place. This book is therefore written in the hope that it will help some teachers or students who work outside of my immediate circle, to make their RE teaching interesting, challenging and real to their pupils.

RALPH R. GOWER
Staff Inspector for Religious Education
The County Hall, London

CHAPTER ONE

The right direction

AN AIM FOR RELIGIOUS EDUCATION

Aims are important.

Unless we know where we are aiming in tennis, football or darts, we are unlikely to win the game. If we did not aim for a series of holes on a golf course, we might end up getting nowhere and achieving nothing. If we do not try to ring the bell on a 'try your strength' machine at the local fair, we have failed to use a means of self-assessment. If we do not aim to get a particular position for our arrow in the archery butts, we lose the motivation to develop particular skills.

Aims are important in playing games. For the same reasons, teachers have become accustomed to setting out their aims when planning children's education. To put it in purely educational terms, a teacher would say that aims are important because they set out clearly what we hope to achieve, and enable the teaching task to be analyzed. Aims provide a means of evaluation of the teacher's work, challenge a teacher to develop particular skills and, by so doing, extend a teacher's performance.

When teachers use the word 'aim' they use it in a

specific, limited, professional way. For a teacher, an 'aim' is what we hope to achieve by the time children complete their education. The aim might be expressed in very general terms, such as 'to develop the ability to fit into society and to make a useful contribution to it'. Or it might be expressed in very specific terms, related to a particular subject discipline which occurs on the timetable of a Secondary school.

Aims for religious education are not normally produced in schools in the same way as aims for history, mathematics and physical education. This is because religious education has a special place in education law. In the case of County schools, the aim for religious education is contained within a document called the 'Agreed Syllabus', which is supplied by the Local Education Authority. It is called an 'Agreed' syllabus because it has been produced by agreement at two levels.

First, there has to be agreement between four committees which represent four sections of the community interested in religious education. They are representatives of the Local Education Authority, teachers, the Church of England and denominations other than the Church of England.

When the four committees have agreed in conference on what religious education should be covered in a particular area, the Education Authority also has to agree with it. In the case of Voluntary schools, that is, schools set up by religious bodies, the aims for religious education are normally laid down by the religious bodies concerned.

If we look at the aims for RE in syllabuses which are used in schools in different Education Authority areas, we find that they often contain similar elements. Some Authorities make a short statement which contains up to three elements. A typical aim will say that when pupils leave school they should know something about religion; they should have come to some kind of decision about it, whether it is for them or not for them; and it should have some effect upon their attitudes to, and relationships with, others.

An aim for religious education put forward by London teachers said:

> (The aim of RE is) 'to enable young people to achieve a knowledge and understanding of religion, so that they are able to come to their own beliefs, and respect the rights of people to hold beliefs which are different from their own'.

In Berkshire, where there are fewer children of other than Christian faiths, the final element is missing. The aim of RE there is:

> 'To help pupils understand religious beliefs, practices and insights in order that they may form their own beliefs and judgements and their own allegiances and commitments'.

Other statements of aim are not always so concise, but the elements are still there. In Hampshire, RE is intended 'to enable pupils to understand the nature of religious beliefs and practices and the importance and influence of these in the lives of believers'. It goes on to say that RE should help children who are 'engaged in a personal search for meaning', and it includes the issue of tolerance by suggesting that RE should 'encourage a willingness to stand imaginatively in other peoples' shoes'. Teachers in Croydon were told 'All children deserve the opportunity to acquire a general knowledge and understanding of religion and the part it can play in shaping peoples' lives. As they grow older, they should be encouraged to develop the skills necessary to evaluate the claims made by religious and other belief systems. They should be helped to appreciate the exciting insights into the fundamental questions of existence which religion offers. They should be equipped with the knowledge and understanding, skills and attitudes necessary to move towards one of the important decisions in life – whether or not to make a personal commitment to some form of religion'.

It is important for teachers to understand the elements of an aim for religious education, and the way that they differ for teachers working within different Education Authority areas because they reflect local conditions and local emphasis. It is for this reason – that local conditions should be taken into account – that the law requires each Authority to decide upon its own syllabus. The details of each element are also of great importance because it is the particular way in which things are put (or are not put) that gives an emphasis to the way religious education is to be taught in a particular area. It is therefore worthwhile for every teacher to look at the aim for RE in his school and to ask important questions of it.

If we take the first, or *knowledge and understanding*, element of the aim, we can ask, 'Does it mention *religion* or *religions*?'

Some people believe that religions are ways that man has used to seek for God, and that it is possible to bring them all together into something called *religion*.

Others believe that there is no such thing as *religion* at all; religion only exists as religions. Each religion is unique and has its own truth claims. It is therefore a mistake to talk about *religion*.

'Does it mention Christianity specifically?' The aims used in many Education Authority areas specifically refer to Christianity and its teachings. This is because Christianity is the likeliest faith to be adopted by children in County schools; it is the basis of our culture and is the heritage of all children. It is said, for example, that unless children come to a knowledge and understanding of the Bible, they are at a disadvantage when coming to study English Literature for examination purposes because so much of our literature is based upon biblical imagery. When one considers our art, architecture, history, customs and legal system, it is clear that children will not find their way about our twentieth-century world without a basic knowledge of Christianity.

For all of these reasons, Christianity gets a specific mention. If Christianity is not specifically mentioned, however, this does not mean that it has no place in the religious education given in the area. It normally means that there are a significant number of children in the area who are of faiths other than Christianity, and it is hoped not to offend them.

'Does it mention faiths of a philosophical type?' Some aims for RE include a statement that children should know about 'non-theistic belief systems' or 'other stances for living'. In the technical use of language within RE, the first is used to include political philosophies, whilst the second involves beliefs which have a positive moral effect on life such as Buddhism and

Humanism. In an Authority where there is a positive Christian approach, such a phrase will often be absent. Other Authorities, however, who stress that religions are only one approach to the business of life, might include such a phrase in the aim.

If we take the second, the emotion or response element of the aim, we can ask, 'What kind of reaction or response are pupils expected to arrive at?'

Some statements emphasize the need for a child to 'decide for himself' about his own beliefs. Other schools emphasize the need for a child to 'make a response' to teaching about religion(s). A statement that a child is to decide for himself normally indicates that those who put the aim into words were afraid of any form of indoctrination. *Response* seems to them to be part of the stock-in-trade of the evangelist rather than the teacher, and they wish to emphasize the educational nature of RE. When the word *response* is used, it is often because it has been recognized that religion involves not only the mind but also the emotions. A child never merely believes: something beyond his mind is touched.

'Whose beliefs are children to come to?'

In Western educational thinking the tendency is to encourage children to examine all religions or approaches objectively and then allow them to make their own decisions. This approach, however, is a completely secular one, because all religious believers believe that their particular faith is the true faith. Leaders of a particular faith, or parents within a particular faith, therefore strongly object to the secularism which is inherent within this movement towards objectivity. They believe that a child needs to be strengthened within his own, incipient faith. Those statements of aim which recognize this are more sensitive to the feelings within religious communities.

If we take the final element of the aim, that of social or moral response, we can ask, 'Is the aim that children be tolerant of other *people* or of other people's *beliefs*?'

There is a very important difference. Many teachers do not believe that it is right for children to grow up to respect beliefs such as Fascism. In the House of Commons debate on the Religious Clauses which preceded the 1944 Education Act, the suggestion was made that religious education should become statutory so that there could be no resurgence of Nazi beliefs in the future. Certain religious leaders would take a similar stance. Orthodox Muslims would not want their children to respect the Christian belief that God actually became human in Jesus. Orthodox Christians would not want their children to respect the Muslim belief that the Muslim Scriptures alone are correct because directly given by Gabriel. On the other hand, teachers are prepared to teach respect for other *people*, even though they may not be able to respect their beliefs. How does the aim for religious education express this issue?

There are many other issues which might be raised about the aim for religious education, but by this time, the reader will have recognized not only that the aim is of great importance, but that the details of the aim need to be spelled out. The teacher of children in the Junior years, however, may ask just how important the aim is at that particular stage.

It may be helpful to compare an RE course with a car journey. Suppose we leave Liverpool and have it as our aim to get to the Isle of Skye. On the way we have to pass through Glasgow. When we are in Glasgow it is here that we have to know the names of the streets, where the one-way systems are and how to avoid the main shopping centre. But while all of these factors are true, it is also important that we know the direction of the Road to the Isles because without it we will not be able to find our way through those things which are important in Glasgow itself. The aim of RE enables the teachers of children in the Junior years to find their way through those things which are particularly important and relevant for Junior-age children.

Or we can look at it using the picture of the building of a house. The finished building is equivalent to the aim, but it cannot be realized unless appropriate foundations – the Infant years – have been laid and unless the first storey – the Junior years – has been completed to plan.

CHAPTER TWO

One step at a time

THE COGNITIVE ELEMENT: KNOWLEDGE AND UNDERSTANDING

The aim of RE is a statement of what the teacher hopes to achieve by the time a pupil leaves school. This aim will give general direction and structure to RE at Junior age in the same way that the knowledge of your destination gives direction on a specific part of a journey, and as the architect's finished drawings give structure to the building of the ground floor of a house. We have seen that an adequate aim for RE has three strands: a cognitive element, relating to knowledge and understanding; a personal element which is concerned with response and linked to the feelings; and a social element which is concerned with relationships with others. We shall now see how each element gives rise to issues which are relevant to children in the Junior age group.

The area of knowledge and understanding has become particularly important in religious education since Ronald Goldman's work in the 1960s. Goldman was aware that the RE of his day had proved to be a failure as far as knowledge and understanding were concerned. Tests taken by children who had undergone a Bible-centred course in Primary and Secondary schools showed that their knowledge and understanding of the subject were minimal.

Goldman was convinced that the reason lay in the fact that children were understanding too much, too soon. He knew from the work of Swiss psychologist, Jean Piaget, that in many areas of the school curriculum there were distinct stages of thinking through which children had to pass if they were to come to mature understanding. He found experimentally that there were stages in the development of religious thinking. There was a period when thinking about religion was extremely limited. At this stage – the pre-operational stage – a child uses himself as a centre of reference, can attend only to one thing at a time and cannot look back on his train of thought. At the following stage, he loses these restrictions, but he is still limited to thinking of religious things in concrete terms. Only at the final, mature, or fully operational stage of thinking can a child abstract, induce, deduce and hypothesize about religion.

The important thing in Goldman's work for Junior children is that he identified the middle stage with the Junior years. This meant that it was inappropriate to use approaches which used metaphor and abstraction. But it also meant that if these methods were attempted with Junior-stage children, then the child would read into the story the literal concrete imagery of his current stage of thinking. This would then set up a mental block which might prevent him from really mature understanding in the future. Goldman believed that this was the reason which lay behind the lack of understanding to be found in Secondary-stage children.

With hindsight we are now aware of some of the limitations of Goldman's work. He isolated the development of thinking from the development of feeling. He equated 'mature' with 'liberal-critical thinking'. His conclusions do not always match his experimental results, and as a matter of fact, some children do not have to wait until they are twelve or thirteen years old to come to the beginnings of mature religious thought. Goldman records a number of instances himself, where children from an evangelical, sect-type, Christian home show a degree of maturity in religious thinking far in advance of what he expected from their chronological age.

This finding is in line with what has been discovered in some other areas of the curriculum. Given a suitably rich environment of language and experience, and appropriate small steps in knowledge, a child's growth in understanding may be accelerated dramatically.

It may have been that Goldman tied his thinking too closely to that of Piaget's. It has been discovered that Piaget's stages are to some extent culturally based. Ages and stages which apply to Western European children do not appear to apply to children of other cultures.

Piaget's stages may also be the result of the particular form and level of language used by adults to elicit children's responses; there is considerable evidence to show that different ages and stages can be found in a different language setting.

Each of the conclusions made point to the same fact – that growth of a child's thinking ability is stimulated by a suitable environment; nurture is as important as nature!

A suitable environment for the development of religious thinking is the experience of religious phenomena, together with the language to communicate about it. Language and experience are always vital in the building up of concepts; religious language and religious experience are vital in the building up of religious concepts.

A teacher in the Junior school must recognize that just as children have different levels of reading, or understanding number, they are likely to have achieved different levels in the understanding of religion. The child from a home with a religious background is likely to have reached a higher level of understanding than the child from a home with no religious background, whose religious language and religious experience is likely to have been limited.

In a religious home, when children experience feelings of wonder in spring time, in looking at mountains when on holiday, in watching baby kittens, or seeing a TV programme on earthquakes, they will have their feelings directed towards God. Words like 'prayer', 'worship', 'hymn' and 'reverence' will have meaning, and can be used. It is therefore necessary for a teacher to draw children without the relevant language and experience into those experiences which are at the root of religious understanding, and to give them the language which will enable them to communicate it.

Many of these experiences may not be religious at all, but they will be part of the child's 'religious education' because they provide a foundation on which a more explicit or obvious form of RE can be built.

This approach is normally referred to as 'Implicit RE'. The term is unfortunate because as used originally it referred to primitive, folk-type religion and superstition. As used in modern RE, however, it is used to refer to the use of everyday experience to provide the grounding for later religious understanding. A child needs to have experiences of power and the appropriate language so that at a later date he will be able to understand the meaning of omnipotence. He needs to have the experience and language of 'I' and 'Thou' so that he can understand the relationships which are part of religious life. Goldman's mistake may not have been in the identification of stages, but in the tying of stages to particular age groups.

While Goldman made the point that information that is too-*advanced* must be avoided, there are others who are concerned lest too *much* information is given. Too much information might lead to confusion. This concern is often expressed in the context of the approach towards world religions in the Primary school. It is felt that if children begin to look at the externals of the major world faiths, they will easily become confused by the terms and ideas. There is evidence that for some children this actually happens; far better then to concentrate on one religion (normally said to be Christianity) so that confusion will be avoided.

There is some basis to the claim that it is better for children to learn first about one area of faith, before following this with wider knowledge. But it does need to be said that the claim that children become confused is not necessarily true. It is a matter of common knowledge that the Junior-age child is a collector – not only of objects, but of bits and pieces of knowledge as well. Junior-stage children collect postcards, stamps and football programmes. But with the stamps they learn the names of the capitals, the currency, the language and the geographical position of each country which issues stamps. Junior children soon become specialist collectors of cards, and they know the history of football and the league tables with greater precision than many adults!

It is certainly not true that all children are confused by many facts. What might be more to the point is that there are occasions when children are faced with facts which do not correspond to their natural interest, while the development of facts into principles through the making of abstractions is too advanced for them. It is necessary for the teacher to be guided by children on such points, bearing in mind that children are individual in development.

CHAPTER THREE

Stand in my shoes

THE PERSONAL ELEMENT: RESPONSE AND FEELINGS

Evaluations of Goldman's work say that he isolated the development of thinking from the development of feeling and so created an artificial situation which does not exist in real life.

There have always been arguments between researchers who have approached the human being by detailed examination of the parts and between those who have insisted on looking at the human situation as a whole. Both approaches have yielded important results in the study of human behaviour, but results obtained when part of human behaviour is isolated from other parts are not necessarily valid for the whole.

This is particularly important in the world of the Junior-age child. A child's world is not broken up into artificial elements; life is seen as a whole. This is recognized in the approach to the curriculum because there is a resistance towards differentiating the field of knowledge like secondary style 'subjects'. 'Subjects' are therefore integrated together as a whole, with children studying aspects of life or 'themes'. While this has implications for Goldman in that he should not have isolated intellectual from emotional development, it also has importance for RE teaching – that it may be a mistake for RE to constitute a separate part of the curriculum.

In normal development, intellect, emotion and social experience are not separated: they grow and develop together. We *learn* the appropriate emotions and appropriate social behaviour. This is why children of limited mental ability often have emotional and social problems; they have not learned to behave appropriately in the social or emotional sphere. It is therefore necessary for emotional development to be considered alongside the development of religious understanding. It is particularly important that it is not forgotten at the Junior stage because here there is a significant development in emotional life.

At the Junior age, children learn what emotional response is appropriate in a given situation, while at the same time they experience more and more forms of emotion. It is because emotions are so much to the fore in this stage that emotional responses are evoked rather than rational ones. There are occasions when this might be not only useful but perfectly right and proper for the teacher. Bissonier has used this approach in the religious education of Roman Catholic children in cases where they are so retarded that it has not been possible to approach them through the rational.

This approach would be strange to teachers in County schools, because the purpose of the work is to bring children *to* faith rather than to inform them *about* faiths. The children are prayed for, and are carefully surrounded by an atmosphere of love and care. They are then given experiences of some of those things which in the Christian faith are key symbols and were used by Jesus. Light and water are two examples. It is claimed that the symbols communicate to the children, that Jesus 'meets the children in the symbol', and that this can be known through the changed response and attitude of the child.

Most teachers would have great reservations about such an approach, not so much because they doubt its relevance to severely handicapped children in a situation of Christian nurture, but because they are conscious of the demands of the teaching profession to avoid such approaches. Education is rational almost as a matter of definition. If a teacher goes beyond the rational, he may be charged with indoctrination. The fear of indoctrination leads positively to the demand for objective teaching. It will be necessary to look into this more closely.

Indoctrination may be defined as any form of teaching which does not properly use a rational approach. One form is to get children to accept, believe or act, not because they understand what they are doing, but because they wish to experience the desirable effects of believing, or to avoid the undesirable effects of not acting. If, for example, Junior-stage children wish to please their teacher, and know that the teacher has personal beliefs which are important to him, the children may adopt those beliefs too, out of a desire to please the teacher. The rational has been completely by-passed by the emotional.

Another form of indoctrination is said to be teaching in such a way that the child cannot change his mind.

This type of teaching is said to be indoctrination because it is supposed to be a sign of rationality that one is always open-minded and never has a closed mind. This approach is somewhat suspect. It would be fatal to be open-minded about the danger of fire or electricity, and it is for this reason that Infant teachers are concerned to make children traffic-conscious before they are fully able to understand the world of traffic. It seems that such an approach may have been labelled with the term because of objection to the phenomenon of religious conversion. Here a person may be so convinced that he has ultimate truth, that there is no possibility of a change of mind!

Other forms of indoctrination are technically suspect as well. It is said, for example, that indoctrination occurs when part of the truth is told as though it were the whole. It is the kind of approach which results from selectivity and is familiar in journalism. The facts are deliberately selected so that while they are true, they do not tell the truth, because they do not tell the whole story. This definition of indoctrination is suspect as it stands, because it is impossible to give the whole truth on almost any situation. What is intended is that whatever is taught should be fair, and balanced.

The fourth view of indoctrination is that it is teaching as *true* things which are not publicly accepted as true. In religious teaching, indoctrination would occur when children were taught as absolute truth that the Archangel Gabriel really dictated the Qur'an to Muhammad. Although millions of Muslims believe this to be true, it is not accepted by everybody to be true. The problem here is probably that nothing could be taught to be true in such a sense.

The positive side of all four aspects of indoctrination is that there is a need for a teacher to be fair and balanced in the way he presents facts, and that care is being taken to treat the child in a way which is true to his humanity. A human being is a rational being: to act as if he is not is to treat him in a less-than-human way.

Another way frequently used to express this is to say that the teacher should be objective, although it does not really mean the same thing. To be objective means to stand outside so as not to be personally and emotionally involved; to look at a thing clinically and dispassionately. It has been suggested that in conducting a class discussion, a teacher should be a neutral observer rather than an active participant. It has been pointed out, however, that in general it is not possible for a person to be a neutral observer in such circumstances; choices of speaker, unconscious inflexions of voice and gesture, all indicate that the most studiously neutral chairman is not neutral at all. Better by far that children know and understand the commitment of a teacher so that they can make their own assessment of a situation and make allowances.

In a more specific sense, it is very difficult to be objective about religion. Religion is about life's basic questions, and because the questions are basic they involve our emotional roots. We cannot be unemotional about the answer to life and the answer to death! Religion is emotional and involves the emotions. If religion were to be taught without emotion, it would not be teaching religion at all.

It is for this reason that it is sometimes said that religious truth is 'apprehended' rather than understood.

It is not emotion which is the problem. Inappropriate emotion is the problem. This becomes all the more important if a teacher has a commitment to a particular religious faith.

In most cases there are two significant things about personal faith. One believes that one has the truth. Each faith is exclusive. Islam claims that its Scriptures alone are inerrant. Christianity claims that 'there is no salvation in any other' than in Jesus Christ. Teachers who have such a commitment cannot be objective about their own faith without their integrity being called into question. They need to be able to say to children, 'This is where I stand'.

The other significant point about personal faith is that it involves a relationship with one's God. One can be objective about a relationship to such a degree that the relationship no longer exists. I can be objective, to a degree, in talking about my wife, but if I were to be totally objective, in comparing experiences of her with those with other women, I destroy the relationship by my disloyalty. To ask a teacher to be totally objective about a love-relationship with his God is to ask too much.

What *is* important is that the teacher is not objective but open – open in the sense that pupils can look into the teacher and see what is there so that they can assess what the teacher says; open in the sense that the teacher does not refuse to listen to another expression of faith or point of view; and open in the sense that while saying 'This is what I believe because of a, b and c', the teacher can also say 'This is what someone else believes because of x, y and z'. If teachers take such an approach, then whatever their commitment, and whatever the decisions of the children they teach in regard to religion, they can know that they are acting in a professionally responsible and acceptable way.

When inappropriate emotion is brought about through the teaching, or if the teaching is not open, fair and balanced, then there is clearly something wrong. Things are also wrong if inappropriate emotion is brought about in the children. Of particular concern are the opposite emotions of 'fight' and 'flight' – aggression and withdrawal. These emotions are often apparent in the life of a child because there is no strong self-concept or self-sentiment.

A self-concept is a child's idea of himself which is built by putting together the pictures obtained from experiences with others. If children know from their parents that they are loved, important, worthy to be considered, and a similar picture of themselves is gained from the teacher, friends at school, neighbours and the leaders of the local youth movement, they will develop strong ideas of themselves as good, worthwhile people. They will have a *positive* self-concept, and will live up to what they believe themselves to be.

If the pictures children get of themselves are inconsistent, however, or if they are all negative so that they feel they are dirty, useless, worthy of punishment and unintelligent, some will live up to the image. Others will fight it and become aggressive, or will accept it and withdraw into themselves. This becomes particularly important for the children of a minority faith group in a majority Christian culture, or for Christian children in a majority materialistic culture. If children are in a position where they feel that they do not count, that their faith is undervalued, that their parents who taught them their faith are ignorant, that they are wrong in their approach to life, they lose the opportunity to become a fully-integrated personality.

A teacher, therefore, has to ensure that the child's personality develops in an integrated way. A teacher who has regard for human personality will not treat a child in any other way.

There is another aspect of emotion which is very important to the child of a minority faith group simply because religion and emotion are always found together. Empathy is a common objective in the Junior school. Teachers seek to help children to 'stand in another person's shoes' so as to imagine what it feels like. Written work and poetry are sensitively used by children to express what they imagine it would be like to be a famous person in history, a child of the rain forests or a hunted creature. Provided that they realize that they are writing imaginatively and not factually, there is no harm done. It is when a child of minority faith is asked to put himself in the shoes of someone of a majority faith, that harm seems to be done, and a child's own faith may be shaken. This is because the rational is being by-passed in an area where, because children are insecure members of a minority, they begin to feel the advantages of being in the majority. It is therefore unwise for a teacher to give the child of a minority faith such an exercise.

CHAPTER FOUR

Love your neighbour

THE SOCIAL ELEMENT: RELATIONSHIPS WITH OTHERS

When London teachers suggested an aim for RE in schools, they incorporated a statement which showed that they expected their work to have a moral effect. Knowledge and understanding were to be acquired, so that 'they will respect the rights of people to hold beliefs which are different from their own'. It is quite common to find a statement about morality built into an aim for RE because religion and morality often come together in human experience. Both are concerned with attitudes, with codes of practice and with institutions.

Teachers have not always been convinced that links between religious education and moral education are a good thing. The view has been put forward that if they are linked together too closely, then the rejection of religion will lead to a rejection of morality. Such a view is laden with value judgements. It is assumed, for example, that while it does not matter over-much if a child rejects religion, it matters a great deal if moral standards are rejected.

The statement is also incorrect in its assumptions. Religion and morality are not so easily separated. While it is possible to have morality without religion – a fact demonstrated by many people who have political or philosophical views which affect their lifestyle – it is not possible to have religion without morality. In New Testament times, James put it very clearly: 'Faith without works is dead'. Unless religion results in better lives and better relationships, it is not worth having. Neither is it possible to separate moral education from religious education. There is much truth in the view that morality has to do with decision-making and that moral education proceeds by helping children to investigate decisions. It is when children ask why it is right to decide one thing rather than the other that they cannot avoid religion, because religion gives answers to life's basic questions. We are therefore justified in looking at moral education as an aspect of religious education.

When teachers discuss moral education it is often said there should not be an 'ME slot' on the timetable because moral education has to pervade every part of the curriculum and school life. On the other hand, there are those who say that it must not be left to chance. Their views reflect two distinct attitudes to ME in schools which are connected with two pieces of research into moral education in schools.

Loukes went into Oxfordshire schools to talk to teenagers about moral values. He found that most of them knew what a 'good person' was, and they knew how to relate ethical principles to problem situations. He found, however, that there was no formal moral education in the schools. What he did find was that in each school there was an attempt made to prevent

corrupting influences, and an attempt to communicate values in the way children were treated by
teachers, in the way they were allowed to participate in
the running of the school, in involving parents, and in
developing a fair disciplinary system. This is to say that
moral education is bound up with the 'hidden
curriculum' and that a child's attitude to moral
standards and practice are affected by the way he sees
such things as selection, pastoral care, organization of
group activities, prefects, rules, rewards, punishment
and community service.

McPhail found that children believed morality
meant taking other peoples' views, feelings and interests
into consideration as well as their own – a kind of
considerate lifestyle. He believed that this was the only
kind of morality which made sense to children, and so
produced materials which could be used to develop such
sensitivities. He suggested that when children received
pleasurable results from such behaviour, it would be
likely to continue. The materials are called 'Startline'
at Primary school level and 'Lifeline' at Secondary
school level. They are sometimes used in English
lessons, tutorial sessions or in RE.

The truth of the matter probably lies in the basis of
all concept development – language and experience.
Formal methods, such as those suggested by McPhail,
provide the language while school ethos and practice
provide the experience. When both combine together
to promote consideration, respect for others and 'love
for our neighbour' there is a likelihood of positive
influence upon the child.

The word 'influence' need not raise the
indoctrination issue again if everybody is agreed on the

content of moral education. There are differences, of course. Even within one faith there can be differences. Some Christians, for example, will allow abortion under special circumstances, while others will not allow it at all; some Christians believe that a nuclear deterrent should be retained, while others are convinced that it is immoral even to possess nuclear arms. Having said this, there are many areas on which most people are agreed – sometimes referred to as 'consensus morality'.

Consensus morality has the twin dimensions of human solidarity and personal autonomy. Human solidarity is expressed in consideration for others, understanding the importance of the needs and feelings of others, and understanding how to help them. Most people would accept this as a very important part of ME. Personal autonomy is expressed in the belief that every individual is important, that no one should be exploited. Every individual should have the freedom to be himself, knowing what restraints there are. Again, most people would accept this is a very important part of ME. A moral education based upon these twin principles is therefore acceptable to the majority.

The difference between the man-made systems of the world is in the *motive* for action rather than in the action itself. A Christian has a different reason for loving his neighbour from the Humanist. It has been suggested that moral education in school should concern itself with the 'what' and that the 'why' should be taught at home. It is easy to see the point of this suggestion. Many teachers, however, would wish to go further in helping children to understand the motivation system which lies behind each faith which they might meet. This is parallel to open religious education.

A morally-educated person should be able to do more than understand the motivational systems of morality and possess a knowledge of what most people believe to be right or wrong. A morally-educated person needs to know what is right for him and have the will to do it. There is considerable debate on how this is brought about. Many people believe that early, fundamental experiences determine our later moral life. There is plenty of evidence that aspects of a culture have a dramatic effect on future moral development. There is a need for children to experience love and affection, to have reasons carefully explained to them when they are not allowed to pursue a course of action, and for them to experience consistent and fair discipline.

None of this is beyond the scope of the teacher. On the one hand the needs can be met in school, and on the other, parents can be encouraged to meet the same needs in the home at the same time – if there are good school/parent relationships. There is also a great deal of evidence that a child's moral development occurs in clearly defined stages. It is important not only that the stages be recognized so that too much is not expected at too early a time, but that reactions to children, particularly in the area of discipline, are related to the development.

Piaget was one of the first to recognize stages in the development of morality when working with boys and girls from Geneva. He believed that morality was the application of rules and therefore studied the way that children applied rules in playing games, in order to find out how all rules, moral included, were applied. He found that after an initial period when there was no understanding of the rules of a game at all (when, for example, young children are given marbles, they do anything with them but play a game of marbles), there were three clearly defined stages.

There was a stage when children obeyed the rules which were given by adults, but then they subsequently moved to a stage where they agreed with other children what the rules of the game should be. Finally a stage was reached where children made up their own rules and imposed them upon others.

There were two things which were inadequate in this work. One was that few people would accept Piaget's idea that morality is the application of rules. The other is that it is limited to the description of stages without any explanation of why one stage gives way to another.

Bull attempted to remedy both defects. He asked West Country children about the behaviour they would expect of people in a number of given situations, such as one where a child sees another child in difficulties in deep water. He found the same three stages of behaviour in conformity with what adults demanded, followed by a stage where children agreed together on appropriate behaviour, and completed by a stage where children made their own decision on the basis of what they believed to be right. Bull did not, however, leave his studies in purely descriptive stages of heteronomy, socionomy and autonomy. He put forward evidence to show that each stage was successively necessary before development could take place to the next level. He also claimed that it was necessary to relate reactions to behaviour to the particular stage of development. Reward and punishment were appropriate for the first stage, praise and blame for the second, and reasoned argument for the stage of autonomy. He has taken us beyond the purely descriptive, but not very far.

It was left to other workers to investigate the processes by which moral autonomy ('I know what is right – and I will do it') is reached, but most ignored the idea of development. Wilson believed that moral behaviour is very complex. Training has to be given in each component of moral behaviour so that it will become possible. He invented his own names for the components of morality which he identified:

- **Phil**, he said, is the ability to identify with others
- **Emp** is the ability to understand feelings
- **Autemp**, one's own feelings
- **Allemp**, the feelings of others
- **Gig** is the necessary knowledge of consequences of action. When a person has these basic skills it is possible to combine them together so that rules for behaviour can be made
- **Dik** is the ability to combine them together to form rules in relation to others
- **Phron** is the same ability directed to one's self
- **Krat** is the ability to act on principles, for principles of action have to be put into action too

Wilson believed that Moral Education consisted of training in the various skills – by discussion, experience, imaginary situations and role play. Hirst had a similar approach, but because he is a rationalistic philosopher, he expresses things differently. Hirst said that to be moral it is necessary to have procedural knowledge – a knowledge of *how* to make rational judgements and to exercise social skills. But we also need to have propositional knowledge – knowledge of our own moral progress, the physical world, other people and so on. We need dispositions to think and to act rationally and we need emotional experiences which will lead to the development of our feelings such that they will support our judgements.

Nottingham has put forward a similar idea in the language of decision-making skills. He says that moral actions are, in effect, decisions. Therefore moral education will proceed as children learn to make decisions. Children are trained by being put into situations in which decisions have to be made, so that they have the experience of bringing values and information together. As children make decisions and thus build up their experience of consequences, they will get feedback which can be put alongside values and information when further decisions are made.

There is a growing body of evidence that feedback from consequences of action is very important in making further decisions. The training involved in these schemes is related to the development of children incidentally rather than directly. It takes time for training to be given, and during that time interval, children grow. Hence the higher level skills are incidentally linked to the older age group. This may not be satisfactory.

Kohlberg linked his scheme of training to the stages of development. Adopting a more sophisticated approach than Bull, Kohlberg looked into the *reasons* which children gave for behaviour rather than their descriptions of expected behaviour. By this means he was able to analyze out the three stages of Piaget and Bull into six steps. He found that progress from one stage to the next was dependent upon the arrangements and attitudes of the next stage being understood by the child before he became hardened at the existing stage of development.

Moral education is therefore more than a natural movement from one stage to the next; it is more than training in skills which are related simply to skills which have already been acquired. Moral education consists of the presentation of ideas and the development of skills which are exactly appropriate for the particular stage of development which the child has reached.

At such a point some people may feel that moral education should not be pursued because the approaches to ME are so diverse. It is not, however, as bad as it appears. The differences are perhaps due to the fact that workers in the field of moral education have dealt only with one aspect of the field, or with one particular phase of development, or because the answers they get result from the fact that different questions have been asked.

There is a sense of pattern about the approaches. It is clear that the atmosphere or ethos of the school is of great importance in moral education because this provides the 'experience' element of concept building. The school must show consideration for staff and children, emphasize the importance of others' needs and encourage children to help others. At the same time the school must show that it considers every individual to be important, that each should develop according to his own potential, and that none should be exploited.

Children at Junior stage will be praised when their behaviour is in line with the ethos of the school: they will get feedback on the results of their actions. They need to be encouraged to make decisions and to act on them. At the same time as the general atmosphere of the school which encourages moral development, there is a need for language experiences too. There is a need for children to put 'a considerate lifestyle' into words. This may come by considering the needs of others, being made sensitive to how one feels one's self in certain situations, and to imagine what it feels like to be in another person's shoes. There is a need for children to know what it is which motivates people to do what is right and wrong and to discover that many people follow the teachings of founders of faiths. There must be opportunities for children to discuss rules with one another and to agree together what is right, and there must be teaching and discussion to move children from what is right for the group to an understanding that when group-interests conflict, it is necessary to be subject to laws which are made for the good of all.

It is perfectly easy for these areas of teaching to be done without any reference to religion at all, but it is not possible to give a complete picture of religion without becoming involved in one or other of these aspects of teaching.

CHAPTER FIVE

An end in view

OBJECTIVES TO BE FULFILLED

What do we actually have to do at the Junior phase of education as far as RE is concerned?

One way might be to make a list of the religious vocabulary which a child should be able to understand and be able to use when leaving the Junior school: vicar, church, Christmas, disciple, prayer, robe, cross, synagogue, Torah . . . (it could be made almost endless). Then those experiences which a child needs to understand the word (concept) should be written alongside. Many of these experiences will be able to be grouped in terms of particular stories, visits, projects, writing, creative work and so on, and it is these particular items which will constitute the syllabus.

A better way is to bear in mind the aim and the interests of children in a particular age group and then frame a set of objectives which will enable the aim to be fulfilled for them. The objectives of a particular school in a particular Authority will differ from those of another school in another place, because the objectives are set to enable children to reach the ultimate aim or destination. If the ultimate aim takes a cognitive, personal and moral form, however, objectives will not differ all that much and they are not likely to vary very much from the set of objectives which are suggested here.

These owe a lot to Dorothy Taylor, who works with me as an advisory teacher in London. They owe a lot to teachers in ILEA who have discussed them as part of their in-service training, and whose reactions continually lead to modification of the objectives. They reflect the approach in a city which has more languages spoken in schools than any other city in the world – a multi-cultural, multi-ethnic, multi-faith city.

What we should be doing: objectives for Primary phase RE

1. To foster feelings of wonder, delight, joy and mystery, and a sense of ritual.

2. To support exploration of the significance of themselves as individuals; as social beings who need to give and to receive and as developing beings who pass through significant stages of life.

3. To encourage a sensitive understanding of the beliefs, attitudes and activities of other people, while helping children to express their own beliefs.

4. To explore ideas with which people have wrestled such as the meaning of life, suffering, the nature of death and the problem of trying to live up to what he believes is right; and to help them cope with painful situations which they encounter.

5. To develop those general capacities such as language skills and the ability to respond to

aesthetic interpretations of life and feelings which may help a child's understanding of religious ideas.

6.   To consider some basic religious concepts such as those which lead to an understanding of the idea of God and the nature of commitment; and ways in which these have been expressed in language and writings, symbols and art, in daily living and in rituals.

7.   To provide knowledge through stories of founders and key figures and their historical and social backgrounds; and of those who have responded significantly to their teaching and lives.

8.   To stimulate a search for knowledge about, and understanding of, activities, rituals, literature and practices of members of particular religious communities.

9.   To give some memorable and 'fun' experiences relating to secular and religious festivals from relevant cultures and traditions through which questions may be asked about the meaning of such occasions.

It would be possible to write a fair-sized book simply on these objectives. They are, however, given as an example of what can be done rather than a prescription to be followed. Nevertheless, there are some very important points to make about them. First, that it is possible to divide the objectives into two fairly distinct groups. The last four are all concerned with recognizable aspects of religion: beliefs, art and symbolism, founders, followers, literature, practices and festivals. They are all concerned with things which most people would associate with religion – the *explicitly* religious.

Many people might think that the first five of the objectives are nothing to do with religion at all; they are simply those things which one would expect to happen in any good Junior school. It is quite true: these things *may* have nothing to do with religion at all, but the point is, if they are not present, there is going to be little point in dealing with the explicitly religious objectives because children will have no background to understand what they are dealing with.

How could a child begin to understand the idea of God (objective 6) unless they know what it is to feel awe and wonder (objective 1)?

How would children understand what it was that made Cliff Richard become a Christian (objective 7) if they have not grasped the meaning of the language with which he describes his experience (objective 5)?

How does a child understand why a Jewish boy-child is circumcized (objective 8) without knowing something of the significant stages of life (objective 2)?

What has sometimes been called 'Implicit Religious Education' is ordinary experience and language which is necessary for explicit religious education to be able to take place. The thing which makes it *religious* is *intention*. When teachers contrive an experience, or capitalize upon a particular situation which has arisen because they know that it is necessary to do this as part of religious education, then it *is* religious education. Religious education does not happen by accident.

The importance for RE of the first five objectives (or similar ones) is that the teacher plans for them or prepares for them. They are not simply left to chance and it is not assumed that a foundation for RE is being laid in the 'general ethos of the school' or in 'standard good practice in the class-room'.

Some Christians, as members of the majority faith in this country, might be concerned about this set of objectives. One of their worries may well be that they feel that 'implicit RE' is watered-down RE. If they mean that it is not easy to *see* the RE, they may need reminding that you cannot normally see foundations, but no superstructure can be built without them. The fact that foundations cannot always be seen does not mean that there is a weakness.

Christians who are concerned in this way are sometimes helped if they recall the nature of revelation and the example of Jesus. The Bible recognizes two aspects of revelation. One is 'natural' revelation, where God is revealed in the universe, in history and in conscience. In Psalm 19, David was able to say:

> 'The heavens are telling the glory of God and the firmament proclaims his handywork'

and later, in his letter to the Romans, Paul was able to say:

> 'What can be known of God is plain to (us) because God has shown it to (us). Ever since the creation of the world his external power and deity have been clearly perceived in the things that have been made.'

'Special' revelation follows this. It is God revealed in Jesus; God revealed in the Bible in order to lead us to salvation. Natural revelation is therefore foundational and prior to special revelation. Implicit religious education is like natural revelation – it is seeing in ordinary experience those things which will make an understanding of the clearly religious experience possible. It is that on which the Holy Spirit works.

Christians also need to recall the example of Jesus. He very seldom started with special revelation: he started with the ordinary experiences of the shepherd, the sower, a lost coin, a king who was going on a journey and people waiting to be hired to work in a vineyard. It is salutary to remember that Jesus rarely began his teaching by referring to the Bible, or by telling Bible stories. Of course, Bible stories have to be known by children as part of their religious education. They would scarcely be literate in a country where Christianity is the majority faith without such knowledge. But stories from the Bible should not necessarily be the mainstay of religious education in the way they have been used in the past.

The position might, of course, be quite different in a church school. Many church schools are known as Voluntary Aided schools, that is, they are not County schools but those set up, voluntarily, by other bodies who provide part of the cost of provision and maintenance of buildings themselves. They are therefore aided by the Government and by the Local Authority. The aid is substantial: 85 per cent of the cost of the buildings, and the entire salary bill, for example. In return for the contribution, the church is, amongst other things, allowed to appoint a Christian headteacher and staff and to provide religious education according to the trust deeds of the school, except in those cases where parents specifically request RE according to the Agreed Syllabus for their children.

If the school is a Voluntary Controlled school, the situation is almost identical to a County school. RE according to the Agreed Syllabus is given, except when parents specifically ask for their children to be taught according to the trust deeds. It might therefore happen that in a Voluntary Aided school the objectives are different because it is the intention that children receive a Christian religious education.

This is not always the case, however. There are some members of the Church of England who do not believe that their schools should be strongholds of distinctive Anglican Christianity. They point out that when church schools were first provided they were intended to meet the needs of all local children and were serving the community, following the tradition of Christian service within the world. They see no reason why there should be any fundamental difference in the present world.

Other members of the Church of England point out that the church has the privilege of being able to advise the Government on education because of its 'established' position. How else can it give an authentic voice in counsel if it does not have a stake in education itself? For either of these reasons, it is not necessary for an Anglican school to provide a distinctive Anglican Christian religious education.

Even if the school is intended to be a Christian school, any form of RE which is given might vary considerably. Some schools practise what has been called nurture – passing on to children a body of revealed doctrine in a supportive way which enables them to accept it. Other schools believe that this is a function of the church rather than the school. RE, therefore, has to be approached rationally and in an open way. It will differ from a County school's provision only in that the starting-point is from within a particular religious tradition. The objectives used in a school depend on which one of the three possible positions is taken. It needs to be pointed out that there would be few, if any, Roman Catholic or Jewish schools which would take the first position, partly for historic reasons, but also because of conviction.

CHAPTER SIX

Focus on themes

APPROPRIATE TEACHING MATERIAL

What teaching material can be used to fulfil the objectives?

The teaching area is normally referred to as a 'theme'. A theme is a centre of interest or focus for teaching religious education. At first sight a theme may resemble a topic, but its purpose is different. A topic is a centre of interest which enables a teacher to bring together skills and related material from different areas of the curriculum. A religious element may therefore be part of a topic. A teacher who is dealing with houses and safety may tell stories about houses as part of the work and include the story of the paralytic let down through the roof in New Testament times. This story then becomes a 'religious bit' of the topic.

Themes are different. They have a wholly religious purpose. They are a centre for language and experience vital for the understanding of religion. Some themes will be obviously (or explicitly) religious in a simple way. They might include 'The Bible', 'Religion in our neighbourhood' or 'Festivals of light'. Others will not look religious at all because they are linked to implicit religious objectives, but they are part of religious education because they provide normal experiences essential for the understanding of later, religious ones. These might include 'Pattern', 'Rules' or 'Barriers'.

Other themes will suggest themselves to teachers because of national or local events which catch the interest of the children, such as 'A Royal Wedding' or 'Processions', while yet more will arise out of things which have happened in school, such as 'Success' and 'Failure' or even 'Fire!' A good teacher is always aware of things which interest children and will see ways of being able to fulfil the objectives through them.

Some themes can be planned in advance, however, because there are many natural centres of interest for Junior-stage children. We could relate eight of our objectives to themes which would make it possible for the objectives to be fulfilled. If a group of teachers were to sit down and draw up a list of themes suitable for Lower Juniors and for Upper Juniors, the list would probably differ from school to school because interests differ. A list drawn up in a school on the coast might differ from a list drawn up in a rural or urban district, for example. A list drawn up by teachers in a Church of England Voluntary school might differ in some respects from a list drawn up by teachers in a County school.

Teachers somewhere, however, might end up with a list looking something like the two tables opposite.

Themes for Lower Juniors

1. TO FOSTER FEELINGS OF AWE, WONDER, JOY AND MYSTERY	Eyes, Pattern, Trees, Weather
2. SIGNIFICANCE OF THE INDIVIDUAL AS SOCIAL AND DEVELOPING BEING	Myself, Friends, Family, Belonging
3. RESPECT FOR OTHERS' BELIEFS	Handicapped people, Eskimos, the local mosque, different lifestyles
4. EXPLORATION OF LIFE'S BASIC QUESTIONS	Fears, New Life, Myself, Light and Darkness
5. BASIC RELIGIOUS CONCEPTS	Bread, Water, Treasure, Love
6. KEY RELIGIOUS FIGURES	Jesus, Abraham, Peter, the Vicar
7. ACTIVITIES, RITUALS AND RELIGIOUS PRACTICES	The Bible, Holy Books, Religious Buildings, Special Clothes
8. CELEBRATION AND FESTIVALS	Harvest, Processions, New Year, Flag Days

Themes for Upper Juniors

1. TO FOSTER FEELINGS OF AWE, WONDER, JOY AND MYSTERY	Space, Power, the Microscope, the Planet Earth

2. SIGNIFICANCE OF THE INDIVIDUAL AS SOCIAL AND DEVELOPING BEING	Responsibility, Sharing, Life Cycle, Achievement
3. RESPECT FOR OTHERS' BELIEFS	Courage, Barriers, Mending, Forgiveness
4. EXPLORATION OF LIFE'S BASIC QUESTIONS	Success and Failure, Good and Evil, Rules, Who am I?
5. BASIC RELIGIOUS CONCEPTS	Signs and Symbols, Fire, Journey of Life, Ideas of God
6. KEY RELIGIOUS FIGURES	Jesus, Moses, Muhammad, Mother Theresa
7. ACTIVITIES, RITUALS AND RELIGIOUS PRACTICES	Service, Local Religion, Initiation, Prayer
8. CELEBRATION AND FESTIVALS	Origins of Festivals, Festivals of Light, Pilgrimage, the Calendar

The themes are not exclusive to particular objectives.
A theme on the microscope may lead to feelings of awe
and wonder, and it may also lead to the question 'Who
am I?' in relation to the world of the infinitely small. A
theme on ideas of God might soon link to other themes
on the nature of power or the way that worship is enacted
locally. A theme on light and darkness might lead to
questions about man's fear of the dark. This might lead
us to believe that in general, the objective and its

fulfilment are more important than the content, but this is not entirely true.

Many parents, and people in society at large, expect a basic content in RE which will enable children to understand our culture. At the Junior stage, this normally means that children are expected to have a basic knowledge of the stories within the Bible, for these lie behind our literature, art, drama, figures of speech, buildings, festivals and customs. If they are not taught in the Junior stage of education, it is even less likely that they will be taught at the Secondary stage. Clearly, a selection has to be made because this is only one part of religious education. There are stories from other faiths and sacred writings which teachers will want to incorporate into their RE teaching at this level. Teachers will use their normal criteria for selection involving plot, theme, characterization, style, appropriateness and theological level. These are explained in some detail in *Religious Education in the Infant Years*, Lion Publishing. Most of the published selections of Bible stories make a suitable start because they have been selected according to similar criteria. The *Puffin Book of Bible Stories* is an inexpensive and good example, but there are many advantages in telling the stories rather than reading them.

What is true of stories from the Bible for all children may need extension into other content for children in church schools. The point has already been made that there are some church schools where it is believed that their purpose is to nurture children into faith; that is, that the school passes on a body of revealed doctrine in a supportive way which enables a child to accept it. Where this is so, the objectives will remain the same but there will be additional, or enriched, Anglican content, sometimes through the provision of alternative themes, and sometimes through additional material within existing themes.

Another issue which has to be raised at this point is that of the school assembly. The 1944 Education Act states that each school day shall begin with an act of worship, but most teachers have one or more reservations about this. These might be expressed as follows:

(a)   Worship is not an activity which can be prescribed. Worship is the expression of heart and mind towards an object of supreme worth, and is therefore sometimes described as 'worth-ship'. The object of worship has to exist before worship is possible: in this way worship is like love. Only those children who have a God to worship can therefore (in the sense that the 1944 Act intended) actually worship.

(b)   In many schools there are children who have different objects of worship. It simply is not true that children of different religions worship the 'same' God. This is a philosophical concept. The character of Allah for the Muslim child is not the same as the character of the Father of the Lord Jesus Christ to the Christian. To try to bring children to a common act of worship is therefore not only impossible, but it can sometimes be subversive of a child's faith.

(c) There is a growing belief among many religious people that worship is so complex an activity that many adults do not themselves achieve worship. It is therefore even less likely that young children will be able to worship. At adult level, one hears this said when a particular group undergo a spiritual experience which makes their worship much more meaningful. They then dismiss the experiences of others as something less than worship. At child level, it has been pointed out that the act of worship involves such activities as adoration, self-orientation, communion, affirmation, ritual and concern, and there is some doubt whether this can be achieved by children.

For these reasons many teachers have moved away from an assembly which is an act of worship, to provide a communal educational experience in which the aims and objectives for religious education are fulfilled. This may be achieved when the headteacher or class teacher uses one of the themes relevant to school life to teach the children, by showing an artefact, telling a story, describing a happening, and so on. It may be achieved when children from a particular class share something about their work or tell the school about things which concern them. It may be achieved when a visitor from outside the school explains the needs of others in the community. There are many, many books on publishers' lists which are intended to provide material for assemblies. Very busy teachers and headteachers often have to rely on them for help, because the pressures of school life make it very difficult to avoid the temptation to use them! Yet if assembly is seen as a place and time where the objectives and content of religious education are used for the whole community rather than for a small teaching group, it will become of greater worth in the life of the school.

CHAPTER SEVEN

Resources

There is an almost infinite amount of material available for the teaching of RE through the objectives which have been suggested. When it comes to the point, however, most teachers appreciate guidance on book resources which are readily available. Individual books come and go, and it is for this reason that a list of well-tried *series* of books is given below. These are linked to the objectives which have been listed in Chapter 5 of this book. An indication is also given of the level for which the series is appropriate (I = Infant; J = Junior; S = Secondary; T = Teacher).

For teachers, there are two books which complement each other and are essential reference books for a teacher who has limited knowledge about religions of the world. *The World's Religions*, Lion Publishing, is a well produced handbook which gives basic information about all of the world's religions, including Christianity. *Religion in the Multi Faith School*, Hulton Educational Publications, provides all that a teacher might need for teaching about world religions, with comprehensive book and address lists.

Objective	Series/Publisher	Examples/Titles	Level
2	People Who Help Us *Young Library*	Mr Kofi is a Doctor Mr Martin is a Postman	J
3	Beans *A. & C. Black*	Boy in Bangladesh Sakina in India Arab Village	J
3	Family in Britain *Religious & Moral Education Press*	A Hindu Family in Britain A Sikh Family in Britain A Muslim Family in Britain	J/S
3	Strands *A. & C. Black*	Nahada's Family Pavan is a Sikh Gypsy Family	I/J
3	How They Live Now *Lutterworth*	Kiku of Japan Rashid of Saudi Arabia Ravi of India	J
3	Unnamed Series (stories of children in multi-ethnic community) *Hamish Hamilton*	Gifts and Almonds Berrow's Tooth	I/J
4	Poems and Pictures *Evans Brothers*	Night Ourselves Miracles	I/J
4	Unnamed Series (children with handicaps) *A. & C. Black*	Clive and Emma Sally Can't See	I/J
4	Unnamed Series (children under stress) *Blackwell Raintree*	Why Did Grandma Die? Mum, Will Dad Come Back?	J

Objective	Series/ Publisher	Examples/ Titles	Level
7	What the Bible Tells Us *Bible Society*	Jesus is Alive Jacob and Esau Jesus and Passover	J
7	Blackbird *Julia Macrae*	Mother Theresa Eric Liddell Mountbatten	J
7	Profiles *Hamish Hamilton*	Pope John Paul Muhammad Ali	J/S
7	Special People *Lutterworth*	Green Book Orange Book	J/S
7	Faith in Action *Religious & Moral Education Press*	Corrie ten Boom Trevor Huddleston Brother Andrew	J/S
7	Stories About Christian Heroes *Winston (US)*	Elizabeth Seton Saint Francis Thomas Dooley	J
8	Beliefs and Believers *Wayland*	Christians & Christianity Muslims & Islam	J/S
8	Friends *National Christian Education Council*	Our Christian Friends Our Muslim Friends Our Hindu Friends	J
8	Understanding our Neighbour *Lutterworth*	Understanding Our Jewish Neighbour Understanding our Sikh Neighbour	J/S

Objective	Series/ Publisher	Examples/ Titles	Level
8	Thinking About *Lutterworth*	Thinking About Christianity Thinking About Islam	T
8	Religions of the World *Macdonald*	The Muslim World The Hindu World	J
9	Living Festivals *Religious & Moral Education Press*	Passover Chinese New Year Christmas	J/S

CHAPTER EIGHT

Examples to be considered

Tom, Bob, Maurice, Elspeth, Jean, Doreen, Margaret
. . . were members of a teachers' group which felt that
staff in Junior schools needed more help in teaching
religious education than they could receive through in-
service training. Problems of day-release, supply cover
and other responsibilities convinced them that each
teacher needed a personal in-service training pack.
They therefore set out to produce a complete set of
teachers' notes which would help teachers to teach RE
effectively, even though they had not received specialist
training to do so.

The notes could start off with objectives, explain any
problems, outline possible content and indicate
resources. The themes for teaching RE at the Junior
stage had already been agreed. The notes were intended
to show one way in which it could be done.

At first teachers were wary: 'Teachers' Notes! –
They went out years ago!!' The first year of use found
teachers following them closely, even slavishly, and they
were limited in their effectiveness because teachers
discovered that they needed to have become familiar
with the resources earlier than they did. By the second

year, resource problems were overcome and teachers knew what was coming. They began to develop their own work with reference to the notes. By Year 3, they had trained themselves, and were using their own approaches to fulfil the objectives.

When a survey was undertaken in schools, it was found that the provision of teachers' notes had been the most appreciated aspect of help in teaching RE at the Junior stage; indeed the notes are now in use in schools in a number of Education Authorities. The work which they produced was closely linked to the children's needs in their schools. Most children came from a Christian-faith background, and there were few children from other cultures. Some aspects of their work, therefore, are not fully relevant to every other area of the country. The importance of their work is that teachers believed that 'it worked' and several units (which are not subject to copyright) are reproduced here as examples of the way some teachers have tackled Junior-stage RE.

The first two units from first year work on bread (7+ to 8+) are closely related. The first is for teachers in County schools and the second for a Voluntary Aided (Church of England) school. Diocese and Education Authority agreed on the themes which should be taught in all Junior schools, ranging from those with an implicit emphasis to those with an explicit emphasis. This was so that when children went on to Secondary schools, they would all have followed the same basic RE programme – a necessity because there were no Church of England Secondary schools. The difference was to be that material for church schools would be 'enriched' with Christian Anglican content. The difference lies in one section of the work. Children in

Anglican schools looked at the sharing of bread and giving thanks for bread, which was linked to the service of Holy Communion. Both units of work take the opportunity to tell Bible stories, and to gain an understanding of the social background to the Bible.

The unit on mending proved to be something of a favourite with most Second Year Junior teachers. It did not have to be confined to an RE lesson, because it involved health education, social education and moral education. There was a strong Christian theme running through the material which teachers found useful as a prelude to teaching about Easter.

The teachers wrote four units of work on Christmas, one for each year in the Junior school. By Year 3, Juniors already knew the story of Christmas, and opportunity is taken in this unit to explore what Christians believe about Christmas through carols and customs. In Year 4, Christmas is developed through the theme of light, when children become familiar with the Hindu festival of Diwali and the Jewish festival of Channukah.

The final unit is from the 4th Year and it begins to look at some of the basic problems of society and of man himself.

These units should not be used in the class-room (unless a teacher feels that they are 'just right' for the situation). They should be examined to see how far they meet the criteria for good Junior-stage RE; to ascertain their strengths and maybe their weaknesses; and as an example and stimulus for preparation of schemes of work for a teacher's own class.

A Unit for Year 1: The Story of Bread

County Schools

1. INTRODUCTION:

a   The objectives of this unit are:

- to enable children to understand the important place that bread has in life so that in due course they will be able to appreciate such phrases as 'the bread of life'
- to enable children to appreciate the co-operative work which is necessary before bread can be produced
- to introduce children to those stories in the Bible which, in being linked to farming, are part of our cultural heritage, and to help them to understand the methods of farming in Bible times

b   Some teachers may wish to use the RE syllabus as a stimulus for a much more general topic on food. If this is done, two books will be found to be very useful. D. Taylor, *Topic Books – Food 2*, Lutterworth Press, 1971, generally approaches things from a 'humanities' angle. D. Kincaird & P. Coles, *Science in a Topic – Food*, Hulton Educational Publications, 1977, is excellent from a scientific point of view.

2. TEACHING CONTENT:
The order is less important than the fact of content.
Many teachers will wish to combine sections together.

a   *Introduction*: In a church or school Harvest
Thanksgiving Service, a loaf of bread, or sheaf of
corn often has a central place. This is because bread
is so basic to life (thus prison fare of bread and water)
that people want to thank God for it.

b   *How we get our loaf*: Ingredients of a loaf – flour,
yeast (leaven) etc; how flour is made; different kinds
of bread and grain; growing different grain (see
Kincaird & Coles, and if available M. Hughes, *The
Importance of Bread*, Rupert Hart Davis, 1966);
grinding the grain – millers and millstones; corn
imported into grain terminal and grown on the
prairies. It is suggested that bread may be made in
class and baked at home, and visits arranged to a
bakery, grain terminal and windmill. Posters are
available from Flour Advisory Bureau, 21 Arlington
Street, London W.1.

c   *Farming in history and in Palestine*: Farming methods
in medieval times (various sections in R. J.
Unstead's history series) and in Bible times –
sowing from basket, trampling with feet, latter
rains, reaping with hand-sickle, gleaning, threshing
floor and threshing sledge, winnowing, grinding
and cooking. (See A. Farncombe, *Food*, National
Christian Education Council, 1977, and R. Gower,
Everyday Life in New Testament Times, Ladybird.
'Daily bread' in Lord's Prayer is a phrase used

because it had to be made daily.) A frieze illustrating old methods of corn-growing may be appropriate.

d   *Bible stories about the corn crop and bread*:

Joseph's storehouses	*Genesis chapter 41*
Manna	*Exodus chapter 16*
Ruth	*Ruth*
The Sower	*Matthew chapter 13*
Feeding of 5,000	*John chapter 6*
The Last Supper	*John chapter 13*

e   *Bread as a Symbol*: Bread is so important that we use the word to stand for any basic food. It is because it is so important that it is often used in religion as a symbol of life itself, and sometimes stands as a symbol of everything for which we give thanks.

3. ADDITIONAL RESOURCES:

E. Owen,   *Lower End Farm*, Blackie, 1978, (tells the story of a West Indian family who settled on a farm)
The Farmer, Ladybird, (description of farm work)

R. Deadman, *Trawlerman*, Blackie, 1974, (introduces the idea of our 'daily bread' being more than bread)

A Unit for Year 1: The Story of Bread

Church of England Schools

1. INTRODUCTION:

a   The objectives of this unit are:

- to enable children to understand the important place that bread has in life so that in due course they will be able to appreciate such phrases as 'the bread of life'

- to enable children to appreciate the co-operative work which is necessary before bread can be produced

- to underline the need to share our food and to give appropriate thanks, and to use this to help children to understand something of the Communion Service in a simple way

- to introduce children to those stories in the Bible which, in being linked to farming, are part of our cultural heritage, and to help them to understand the methods of farming in Bible times

b   Some teachers may wish to use the RE syllabus as a stimulus for a much more general topic on food. If this is done, two books will be found to be very useful. D. Taylor, *Topic Books – Food 2*, Lutterworth Press, 1971, generally approaches things from a 'humanities' angle. D. Kincaird & P. Coles, *Science in a Topic – Food*, Hulton Educational Publications, 1977, is excellent from a scientific point of view.

2. TEACHING CONTENT:

a   *Introduction*: In a church or school Harvest Thanksgiving Service, a loaf of bread, or sheaf of corn often has a central place. This is because bread is so basic to life (thus prison fare of bread and water) that people want to thank God for it.

b   *Farming in history and in Palestine*: Farming methods in medieval times (various sections in R. J. Unstead's history series) and in Bible times – sowing from basket, trampling with feet, latter rains, reaping with hand-sickle, gleaning, threshing floor and threshing sledge, winnowing, grinding and cooking. (See A. Farncombe, *Food*, National Christian Education Council, 1977, and R. Gower, *Everyday Life in New Testament Times*, Ladybird. 'Daily bread' in Lord's Prayer is a phrase used because it had to be made daily.) A frieze illustrating old methods of corn-growing may be appropriate.

c   *Making Bread*: Ingredients of a loaf – flour, yeast (leaven) etc; how flour is made; different kinds of bread and grain; growing different grain (see Kincaird & Coles, and if available M. Hughes, *The Importance of Bread*, Rupert Hart Davis, 1966); grinding the grain – millers and millstones; corn imported into Seaforth terminal and grown on the prairies. It is suggested that bread may be made in class and baked at home, and visits arranged to a bakery, grain terminal and windmill. Posters are available from Flour Advisory Bureau, 21 Arlington Street, London W.1.

d   *Sharing Bread*: Sharing of food and the giving of
thanks associated with it have an important place
among Christians.

- Family meals together are preceded or followed
  by 'saying grace' or giving thanks. (Children
  may wish to compose a suitable grace.)

- Family celebrations such as baptisms and
  weddings are followed by a meal when people
  share in the happiness together, and write
  'thank you letters' afterwards.

- The world-wide family of man needs us to
  share our bread (thus the words of the Lord's
  Prayer, 'Our Father . . . give *us* each day *our*
  daily bread' and this results in thanksgiving).
  Note work of missions.

- The Christian family meets to share in Christ's
  work for us in the Communion, and it is a time
  for fellowship and thanksgiving (Eucharist).
  Juniors should be able to *describe* what happens
  at the service, and to know the geography and
  furniture of the church even if they do not,
  themselves, communicate.

In some parishes it might be possible to celebrate
Communion in the school.

e   *Bible stories about the corn crop and bread*:

Joseph's storehouses	*Genesis chapter 41*
Manna	*Exodus chapter 16*
Ruth	*Ruth*
The Sower	*Matthew chapter 13*
Feeding of 5,000	*John chapter 6*
The Last Supper	*John chapter 13*

f   *Bread as a Symbol*: Bread is so important that we use the word to stand for any basic food. It is because it is so important that it is often used in religion as a symbol of life itself, and sometimes stands as a symbol of everything for which we give thanks.

3. ADDITIONAL RESOURCES:

E. Owen,   *Lower End Farm*, Blackie, 1978, (tells the story about a West Indian family who settled on a farm)
The Farmer, Ladybird, (description of farm work)

R. Deadman, *Trawlerman*, Blackie, 1974, (introduces the idea of our 'daily bread' being more than bread)

A Unit for Year 2: Mending

1. INTRODUCTION:

a There are a number of objectives here: to help children to realize that when things are broken, there has to be more than an expression of sorrow – something needs to be done to put things right; to help children to understand the experiences of being forgiven and the necessity to forgive others; to encourage responsibility to protect and preserve things of value in the life of a community.

b Although it can be taught at any time, this unit has been written with the thought that it is appropriate during the Spring term, to precede work done on Easter. It is related to work on caring (Year 1: Unit 2) in a number of ways.

c It has been found that, M. Pugh, *Mending*, Leprosy Mission (50 Portland Place, London W1N 3DG), 1977, is a most useful resource as a set of teaching materials for this unit and is very reasonably priced. It is of much value to the teacher.

d The caring attitude of the school itself in seeking to mend broken relationships is an essential foundation to the successful teaching of this kind of unit.

2. TEACHING CONTENT:

a *Broken Things*:

- Toys get broken and things get broken at home and at school. The person it belongs to is always very sorry. But it is not enough to be sorry. The watch has to go to the jeweller's, the TV to the engineer, the glazier has to mend the windows, the tear has to be sewn. It is only when things are mended like new that we begin to feel better again. We can prevent this by taking care of things.

- Buildings, street furniture and parks sometimes get 'broken' too – by vandalism. When this happens, people get upset too (caretakers who keep a building clean and tidy, gardeners who look after flower-beds, people who look after their houses) and they get hurt too. Many children are treated in hospital because of falls on broken glass and tripping over litter. Elderly people are hurt by tripping over old bricks, and lonely people get afraid. Children need to prevent these things from happening by taking active pride and interest in the appearance and general care of school buildings and class-rooms.

(Some people might want to ask the school caretaker and cleaners to talk about their work and explain how children can help. Encourage children to talk about their experiences. How can they put things right when they break things belonging to others?)

b *Broken Health*: We sometimes say that health is

'broken' when a person is ill and it takes them a long time to get better.

- It is possible that bodies need mending because they are not looked after properly. We can, for example, eat too much, eat too many sweets, neglect dental treatment, have insufficient sleep or exercise (the children can be drawn on these, but the Schools Council Health Education Project materials, *All About Me* and *Think Well*, Thomas Nelson & Sons, have useful resources, especially if this unit is linked to health education). How can we best look after the body which has been given to us?

- When health is broken, who helps us to get better? Try to draw out the three answers – parents, doctors and nurses, God. Get the children to explain how each plays their part in helping them to get well. Put special emphasis on parents as they are often taken for granted. (Younger children may play doctors and nurses: write prayers for assembly for doctors and nurses and people in hospital.)

- When Jesus lived there were very few doctors, and those there were (like Luke who wrote the Gospel) did not have the knowledge that doctors have today and helped only those wealthy enough to pay for treatment. Jesus therefore helped as many people as he could to make them well, e.g.

The leprosy sufferer	*Luke 5:12–15*
The cripple	*John 5:19*
Blind Bartimaeus	*Mark 10:46–52*
A deaf and dumb man	*Mark 7:31–37*

c   *Broken Relationships*: We can break friendships with people, or 'break relationships'. When that happens somebody is always hurt. When *that* happens there is a need not only to be 'sorry' but to give and receive forgiveness.

- Relationships which go wrong in children's lives – with parents, brothers and sisters and friends. (Draw these out from children. Divide class into groups and get each to make up a scene where there is a quarrel. Then discuss with children what went wrong and how the relationship can be mended.)

- Stories of relationships which went wrong and how people were forgiven. e.g. Joseph (especially if the children know 'The Amazing Technicolour Dreamcoat'), the altar in the ruins of Coventry Cathedral – 'Father Forgive', the disciples' quarrel as to who should be the greatest (*Genesis 37f; Luke 22: 24–27*). Emphasize that Jesus taught that we *should* forgive one another: The Lord's Prayer, the Unforgiving Servant (*Matthew 18: 21–34*) and forgave people himself. Jesus forgave Peter (*John 21*).

- Jesus mended lives which were broken – by helping people to put things right. The story of Zacchaeus (*Luke 19:1–10*) is probably the best example. Some children may also begin to understand that we break relationships with God when we break his laws (*Exodus 20:1–17; Luke 10:25–28*). Jesus came to show us how to put things right with God.

A Unit for Year 3: Christmas

1. INTRODUCTION:
The aim of this unit is to use the child's natural interest in the customs of Christmas to help him to understand what the customs are expressing and through this understand what Christians see as significant about Christ. At the same time, more able children will begin to understand the nature of symbolism in religion and may be able to develop their own symbols to express what Christmas means to them.

2. TEACHING CONTENT:
a   *Introduction*: Explain that Christmas is the time when Christians celebrate (mass or mas) Christ's birthday – hence the name of the festival. Find out ways that children in the class celebrate Christmas as an introduction to systematic teaching about customs.

b   *The Customs of Christmas*:
  ● Christmas in this country in the past
    Before Christmas began; pagan festivals of winter time
    King Arthur at York
    the Puritan Christmas
    the Victorian Christmas (C. Dickens, *The Christmas Carol*)

  ● Christmas as it is kept in this country today
    lights and candles
    crib and nativity play

carols (what new ones are there as well as traditional?)

evergreens and decorations

gifts and Santa Claus

cards

food and feasting

the pantomime

the twelve days of Christmas

St Stephen's Day

Boxing Day

(RESOURCES: At children's level there are two useful books: N. Pearson, *The Stories of our Christmas Customs*, Ladybird, 1964, and E. Blyton, *The Christmas Book*, Piccolo. The first is systematic and the second deals in story form with questions raised by children in a family. Shire Publications publish a booklet of *Christmas Customs* by Margaret Baker and many other firms produce omnibus-type books which include craft work, carols, stories, etc., e.g.: S. Baker, *The Christmas Book*, Macdonald Educational, 1978, and T. Tudor, *Take Joy*, Lutterworth, 1967. Such books become an annual publishing event.)

● Christmas customs around the world
An excellent resource book for *teachers* which includes legends, international Christmas recipes, a suggestion for a school presentation etc., as well as international customs, is H. H. Wernecke, *Christmas Customs Around the World*, Bailey Brothers & Swinfen, 1974; probably the best resource book in general on Christmas for

teachers is W. Sansom, *Christmas*, Weidenfeld and Nicholson, 1968, (both books available from the Library Service).

- Christmas carols around the world.
  A collection of sixty-one international carols in simple notation, all singable by Juniors, is available: R. Heller, *Carols of the Nations*, Blandford Press, 1955.

c *The Meaning of the Customs*: This is one of the most important elements of the material. The customs are intended to lead to this end.

- One of the overwhelming impressions is that of great *joy*: 'Joy to the world . . .' Something happened at Christmas which made people want to be joyful and to try and make other people joyful by things that they did – feasting, giving, laughter, brightness, in a drab time of year, etc.

- Many of the customs and carols show what it was that Christians were joyful about: nativity plays and carols – God sent his Son to this world
  light – he came to dispel our darkness and ignorance
  evergreen – he came to conquer death and fear
  incorporation of pagan festivals – he came to show us the *real* way
  giving – he came to make us happy

Adults might put it that Jesus was God's answer to the problems of mankind.

d *Our own symbol*:

- The Christingle: The Church of England Children's Society has revived an old custom and renewed it in 1968 in Lincoln Cathedral, as a means of raising funds as well as emphasizing the 'Christ light' of Christmas. During the service, each child is given an orange to symbolize the world, into which is stuck a candle. Around the orange are four cocktail sticks on which are placed nuts, raisins, small fruits and sweets – the fruits of the earth. The final touch is a red ribbon representing Christ's death. This service is held at the beginning of Advent. It is possible to purchase a pack from the Society (Old Town Hall, Kennington Road, London SE11 4QD).
- Can the children think out their *own* way of expressing what Christmas means to them in symbolism and then present their ceremony to the school?

A Unit for Year 4: Rules

1. INTRODUCTION:

a   The objectives for this unit are: to help children to understand why rules and regulations are important, and to know some of the basic rules so that they might be more willing to adopt a more responsible attitude. By coming to an understanding of why it is difficult to keep rules it is hoped that children might become aware of the basis of beliefs that Christians hold about the nature of Christianity.

b   The point of view taken in this unit is that the keeping of rules is a social convenience. Rules help us to get along together, they keep us out of danger and they tell us what is expected of us in society. While this is adequate for 4th Year Junior level, it needs to be realized that there is more to rules than this. Some rules are made to maintain a power structure, for example.

2. TEACHING CONTENT:

a   *Introduction*: A look at some of the rules and regulations which we are expected to keep. A start can be made either with a list of rules which are subsequently analyzed, or else with a list of types of rules which are exemplified in actual rules. Mention should be made of:

- social rules — Guide and Scout laws, rules of games, use of library
- local rules — parking, highway code, country code
- school rules — use local examples
- church rules — Ten Commandments (*Exodus 20:1–7*), the Great Commandment (*Matthew 22:34–40*), Christ's examples (*John 13:15*)
- national rules — how laws come into being, the Magna Carta, the Magistrates' Court
- home — domestic rules of helping, e.g. Samuel listening to Eli (*I Samuel 3*)

Some teachers may wish to use stories which give examples of obedience in a Christian context, e.g. obedience of disciples (*Matthew 4:18–22*); Saul's obedience on the Damascus Road (*Acts 9:1–9*); Paul telling the Romans that they should obey the Government (*Romans 13:1–7*); Jesus defining our obedience to God and Caesar (*Matthew 22:15–22*).

b *Why do we have to have rules?* Help children to realize that there are three very important reasons:

- to regulate society – without rules, games would be impossible, nobody could depend on anyone else, trains could not be caught, etc.
- to protect people – e.g. highway code, trespassing on the railway, playing with firearms. What dangers would we be in if there

were no rules? Rules are also to protect people
who might get hurt by us.

●   to help us to act responsibly. The rules we are
given are those adults know are needed so that
we will grow up to consider other people. If we
did not know how best to live, then as we got
older we would cause chaos in society. Society
has therefore made sure that there are people
who teach us our responsibilities. E.g.
teachers, policemen, ministers, magistrates,
parents, etc.

c   *Why do we find it difficult to keep rules?* Look over the
rules which children find it difficult to keep. Why do
we find it easier to break rules than to keep them?
It is basically because we are all *selfish*. Rules are
needed so that not only do we know what we should
do, but so that we begin to realize the problem of our
own selfishness. If there were no rules and we could
do what we liked, we would not realize how selfish
we were. Even when we do know what rules there
are, it is not easy to keep them. Some people believe
that rules can be kept by making a special effort.
Christians believe that it is necessary for God to help
them keep his rules – and they would say that a
Christian is a person who does receive God's help
because they have asked for it.

3. RESOURCES:
G. Mabbut, *Topic Books* – *Laws*, Lutterworth, 1971

CHAPTER NINE

The future of religious education

We have completed a course in which we have considered an aim and objectives for religious education and we have investigated some of the professional matters which they lead to. We have looked at possible themes through which religious education can be taught and have identified some teaching materials which can be used. We have also looked at approaches which a particular group of teachers have used in interpreting the theory of the course. The remaining question is 'Will it succeed?' or more bluntly, 'Is there any future for RE?'

There seem to me to be three major factors which are involved in the future of religious education.

1. RE will become more difficult to teach. Although religious education is required by law, there is a large number of schools where 'lip service' alone is paid to it. This is because its presence on a school time-table tends to be related, not to the law, but to whether or not its presence can be justified on educational grounds. If RE survives today, it is because the head teacher is convinced it is of value

to the pupils in the school. How would a head-teacher be convinced? In practice it has been shown that there are three basic arguments which convince professional teachers that religious education should be included in the curriculum.

(a) The 'nature of Man' argument. All human beings are concerned with the basic questions of our existence such as, 'Why am I here?' 'Where am I going?', 'What is the purpose of life?', 'What is the nature of right and wrong?', 'Will it affect the way I die?' 'Does it matter anyway?' and so on. The area of the curriculum where such issues are dealt with is religious education, because all religions have addressed themselves to those questions. RE therefore becomes an essential part of a child's education.

(b) The 'need-to-understand-one-another' argument. We live in a world in which religion has been and still is of great importance. Religion is one of the aspects of the culture of many millions of the world's people. Moreover, most people feel very deeply about their faith and it is for this reason that religion lies behind many of the world's conflicts. The conflicts between Iran and Iraq, the Arab states and Israel and the communities in Northern Ireland can be better understood with a knowledge of the religious beliefs involved. Tensions on global or national scale can arise locally where people of different faiths live together. Understanding each other's beliefs and practices lifts the threshold of tolerance so that it becomes more possible to live together in harmony. It is therefore important that children come to a knowledge and understanding of world faiths.

(c) The cultural arguments. There are a number of elements which make up a particular culture – ethnicity, language, history, custom and religion, for example. We can only come to an understanding of an existing culture by investigating each of these elements. The culture of the United Kingdom has a very important religious element. Our art, literature, architecture, legal system, customs and even our language, to some extent, are rooted in Christianity. It is only as children understand something of the Christian faith, that it is possible for them to 'find their way about' our culture.

There are other arguments for the inclusion of religious education within the school curriculum, but those are sufficient to make the point. Not only do such arguments state the case for including RE: they also shape the kind of RE which has to be given. These arguments can only be used if religious education is to become philosophical, related to world religions and to bring about an understanding of Christianity in our own country.

This is not an easy programme to put before a teacher. Each teacher needs to have grappled with the question of existence, be aware of what has been called philosophical introduction to theology, has to have a working knowledge of the major world religions, (which includes Christianity) and to know something of English church history. This is more than has ever been asked of teachers in Junior school in the past. Very few teachers would take RE as a major element in their initial training and only this would enable them to carry through such a programme.

It seems quite likely therefore, that if RE remains a statutory obligation, and if it is to be justified on educational grounds, there will be a need to train RE specialists for the Junior school. These teachers will become a centre of reference within the school, be responsible for school-based in-service training of colleagues and will assemble the resources colleagues will need for teaching. It will also be necessary for such teachers' expertise to be recognized by the allocation of a 'graded post' for RE within each school, in the same way as such posts are often given for language, games or music.

2. RE will not be a popular area of the curriculum. It is probably true to say that RE has never been very popular. If trends within society at large and within school curricula continue, it is likely that it will become less popular in the future.

Research which has been done into childrens' attitudes to religion has shown that there is a decline in interest with age, and that this is more marked in boys than in girls. Studies undertaken in Eastern England seem to show that the decline is less acute in Roman Catholic schools than in County and Church of England schools. The process is accelerating, however, and the level of interest was low to start with!

There may be much truth in the response that RE has always been a Cinderella subject — that when it first became statutory, teachers were expected to undertake it although no supplementary training and totally inadequate resources were provided. The situation has never been remedied. My immediate concern, however, is that there is a likelihood that the negative attitude towards the subject will become sharper. This is for three reasons:

(a) Materialistic Outlook. Our society is slanted towards concern for material things. This is all that matters: there is nothing (worthwhile) other than the material. It is reflected in a policy which places material profit above the dignity of human labour so that unemployment increases in the cause of efficiency. It is inherent in the comment of a child to the form tutor 'Why do I need to do RE? It won't get me a job. I don't want to be a vicar'. It is the reason why so many of the leaders of the Muslim faith and some groups of churches have attempted to set up Muslim or Christian schools where their children will not be so exposed to the materialistic climate of our society. It is the fact which lies behind the overall decrease in church attendance which has been going on for decades.

In such a society, anything which grapples with the fundamental questions of man is unwelcome, because it challenges the presuppositions on which our society is based. Any subject area which examines the beliefs and practices of religious people is believed to be irrelevant. Not only is RE irrelevant as far as children are concerned, but it is felt to be irrelevant to teachers and to parents. Their attitudes, even if not conveyed by words, are not lost on children and, as a result, the subject is unlikely to become popular.

(b) Technological emphasis. As part of a society which is seeking to maintain its (material) place in the world, we are experiencing a 'second industrial revolution' as we move towards high technology. Human labour has become so costly that it has become necessary for replacements to be found in the form of the silicon chip. In order that children may grow up naturally into a technological society, central government has given assistance so that many Primary schools have been able to install a computer. To some extent, this has proved necessary to demonstrate the relevance of education. More homes in the UK have a home computer than in any other country in the world.

Today's children 'think computers' – it has become a natural part of their growing up. So much is this true that many tend to think that if they cannot relate the computer to subject areas of the curriculum, then the subject area is irrelevant. It is relatively easy to produce computer software related to science, mathematics, geography, design and technology. It is much more difficult to produce it for a subject like religious education. Attempts have been made to produce games which demonstrate the battle between good and evil and to make children decide on a path of action which involves them in certain consequences but it has proved extremely difficult to devise programs which involve philosophy and which give basic information about religious faith. If a computer is used as a means of retrieving information, it is simply using an expensive tool for what can be achieved through a well-designed book. Unless these problems can be overcome speedily, it is likely that RE will be relatively less popular than those subject areas which easily relate to computer programs.

(c) Content importance. One of the reasons for difficulty in connection with the computer is that religious education is much more concerned with content than some other areas of the curriculum. In history teaching, for example, it has become more important to teach children the skills so that they can find the facts for themselves.

This cannot be entirely true for RE. If religious education is to bring about mutual understanding, the understanding has to be achieved through facts. If we are to consider the answers given by religious faith to the basic questions of life, we have to know both the answers and the faiths which generated them. This makes it very difficult for religious education to be joined with other subject areas in the way that 'cross subject-teaching' is normal for the Primary school. Refer back to the list of objectives in chapter five. The final, explicit RE objectives often have to be taught in isolation from other subjects. This does not endear the subject area to teachers who use their skills to bring different areas together.

3. RE needs well-trained teachers. They need not only to be well-trained themselves but have the ability to equip their colleagues to teach RE too. Whether or not this is possible will depend upon the provision of places to train such teachers, and upon the willingness of young people to come forward to take up the places.

(a) Facilities for training. Central government controls the total number of places available for teacher training and also the particular courses to be run. This is so that (in theory) there will always be the right number of teachers for the right age groups and the right subject areas.

   People can train to be teachers in two ways. They can enter a College of Higher Education and do either a three or four-year course. This would consist of three units: Education (including three periods of practical experience), Main Subject (science, mathematics, art, history . . . RE) and a number of short courses which together make up some kind of Professional Studies. The latter includes the basics of the other subjects, and elements such as teaching in a multi-ethnic society, language across the curriculum . . . taking a school assembly and so on. Unless a teacher undertaking initial training deliberately opts for training in religious education, then, despite the fact that in a Primary school all teachers have to teach religious education unless they legally decide not to do so, the majority will have no training to do so whatsoever.

Others take a first degree and then go to a University or Polytechnic Department of Education to take a Postgraduate Certificate in Education. Again they undertake education studies with teaching procedure, and normally take a 'main' teaching subject and supplementary units. The grim fact which we have to face at present is that central government has continually cut down the number of RE courses which are available for the training of RE teachers. There are not even sufficient places to train specialists for Secondary schools, let alone specialists for Primary schools. This cut-back has been continually and consistently opposed by the Religious Education Council, and teachers who wish to purchase an account of the statistics involved can always write to Dr Brian Gates at St Martin's College, Lancaster, who monitors the situation on behalf of the REC.

Unless people recognize the need (and the danger) of the present situation and can convince central government of the need to provide more places, then there can be no adequate training for the teaching of religious education.

(b) Provision of teachers. There are two factors which influence whether or not a student in the sixth form or a College of Further Education will decide to become an RE teacher. In the first place, there is what I would call 'external motivation'. If a pupil or a student is interested in RE in school, then he might be motivated to train to teach religious education.

To a large extent this depends upon the skill and enthusiasm of the school's RE teacher. Unfortunately, because central government has failed to ensure an adequate number of RE teachers by restricting the number of places available for training, headteachers and governors have found RE teachers in short supply. They have therefore been forced either to employ non-specialists, many of whom lack the knowledge and skills to make RE interesting, or they have had to make RE part of 'Integrated studies', Life skills' or 'Humanities', which in many cases means that it is hardly taught at all. Not only does this prevent people and students from receiving enthusiastic teaching, but it devalues the subject in their eyes. Consequently, the 'law of diminishing returns' operates and fewer and fewer students opt to become RE teachers.

In the second place, there is what I would call 'internal motivation'. This is where a person has found that their faith means so much to them that they want to help other people to find faith too. In the years following the 1944 Education Act and before concern about indoctrination made it professionally impossible, many Christian students trained to become RE teachers because they wished to teach others about the Christian faith. It is important to recognize that even in the 1980s, over 50 per cent of those who apply to local authorities to become RE teachers are still Christians. There are increasing numbers of those who profess no particular faith, and a few of the Jewish faith, but there is almost none outside of this. The Christian church still provides the majority of RE teachers. The fact that the proportion of Christians coming forward is declining might indicate that they are less certain today that they should be involved in RE teaching. Only if they can be convinced, will there be a future for religious education.

Christians and religious education

We have to turn finally to a Christian perspective on RE. Why are some Christians asking whether teaching RE in its current form is a suitable occupation for them? Those who look at the problem from a Christian standpoint must realize that they are not alone. All religions have unique truth-claims. All believers face the same type of problems. With this proviso, let us look at some of them.

(a) The problem of disobedience. Some Christians argue that Jesus told his followers to preach the gospel and RE is a means of doing this. To be an RE teacher when one cannot preach the gospel is to be disobedient to the command of Jesus. This argument is not a logical one on two counts. If RE was the *only* means of preaching the gospel, and if Christians were to do *nothing but* preach the gospel, there would be some logic in the argument. But neither of those statements is true. A Christian mathematics teacher would not expect to preach the gospel while undertaking teaching about volume or solids. There is no necessary reason why a Christian should preach the gospel while teaching about the major religions of the world and their effect in the lives of adherents.

There are two things which can always be true for a Christian: he will be able to demonstrate the presence of Jesus in his life and he will be able to take an active part in evangelism through his church. The last point is important. It is as Christians in churches understand the current trends in religious education that they will be able to take account of them in their outreach to the community which they serve.

(b) The problem of objectivity. Some Christians are concerned that they are being untrue to their faith when they are required to be open and objective about *all* religious faiths. They feel it denies the relationship they have with God if they are objective about the life and death of Jesus.

No teacher from any faith is expected to be objective about it in a way which threatens his own faith. Indeed, it is recognized that such a degree of objectivity would be impossible. Teachers of any faith should be allowed to let children know where they stand. Children can then make the necessary adjustments in assessing what their teacher says and does. This is perfectly in order, provided it is not used in such a way that it might persuade children to identify with their teacher's faith.

(c) The problem of disloyalty. Other Christians may feel that if they teach about other religions besides their own faith, then not only is this disloyalty but it may prevent children from finding what they consider to be the Truth. This problem is not one which is unique to Christians. Any believer who believes his faith has unique truth-claims feels the same way. Yet if Jesus is God, if he is alive today, if there is nothing and none other who can compare with him, if his word is truth, then everything else pales into insignificance when placed beside him. What fear could a Christian teacher have of teaching about other faiths when such an approach would demonstrate where the truth really lies? The supposed problem of disloyalty is no reason for Christians to refuse to be involved in a multi-faith religious education.

It is to be hoped that Christians will continue to come forward to train to become RE teachers and RE specialists in the Primary school years.

Conclusion

It appears that religious education could be entering yet another difficult phase. It will become more and more difficult to teach, because on the one hand the content will become increasingly more demanding, and on the other hand, the general trends in our society are likely to make many children unwilling to take the subject seriously.

Neither of these things need be a disaster; teachers are used to facing challenges to teaching and to meeting the challenges in full. Besides, social trends do not have to continue. National and international events can concentrate the minds of parents and children on the basic questions of our existence and bring home the importance of mutual understanding. There have been and there can be times of spiritual revival within the nation. The real problem lies in the provision of teachers – that the need is taken seriously by central government, and that, in the full knowledge of what is involved in religious education, young people continue to come forward to teach it.

ACKNOWLEDGEMENTS

When I wrote *Religious Education in the Infant Years* I was to a great extent protected from my own ways of expressing things and my way of jumping in 'with both feet' by writing the book with six other people. I had no such protection when this book was written. It arose from a seminar given to educational representatives who wanted to know enough about RE so that when they approached teachers in school, they could at least do so with some coherence! The faults in the book are therefore entirely my own.

But at the same time I owe a very great debt to a large number of people because they have been prepared to argue with me and challenge my views, and others have been willing to try out the principles for themselves. As a Junior school teacher herself, my wife, Margaret, has tried out many of the lessons and has encouraged me to make the 'theory' available to others after sitting in on one of my courses. The teachers who worked with me to produce the 'notes' were all from Sefton Education Authority in Merseyside where I spent many happy years. The challenges have come from some of the permanent members of the Religious Education team in London (ILEA) and I have been especially grateful for the stimulus which has resulted from Dorothy Taylor (Primary Advisory Teacher), George Oliver (Inspector) and Arthur Rowe (RE Centre Warden). They still may not agree with all I have written, but they will see the points in this book where they have been influential in making me think again.

To them all, I acknowledge my debt and give my thanks.